The South was Right, by S. A. Steel

# The South Was Right

BY S. A. STEEL

COLUMBIA, S. C.
THE R. L. BRYAN COMPANY
1914

# The South Was Right

## BY S. A. STEEL

COLUMBIA, S. C.
THE R. L. BRYAN COMPANY
1914

# FOREWORD

I dedicate this work to the young Americans of today. It is a statement of the reasons which led the Southern States to withdraw from the Union in 1861. These reasons are given more fully in many large works, but our young people never see them, and the average man is too busy to read them. Northern writers have never understood our side, and even when disposed to be friendly, are incapable of interpreting our motives. Most of the histories used in our schools are too brief to give a correct idea of the subject, yet it is very important that it should be understood. I have endeavored to put the most important facts in a brief space and simple form, with the hope that they will be read by people too busy for larger books, and especially by pupils in our schools and colleges. I believed in the beginning of the war, though only a child, that the South was right, and I believe it now. And I believe further that if this government lasts a hundred years longer, and continues to be a nation of free people, it will be because the principles of political liberty, for which the South contended, survive the shock of that tremendous revolution. For this reason, if for no other, the position of the South should be understood.

Columbia, S. C. S. A. Steel.

"I maintain that if the issue of this struggle had from the outset been manifest to the whole world, not even then ought Athens to have shrunk from it, if Athens has any regard for her own glory, her past history, or her future reputation."—*Demosthenes.*

"We had, I was satisfied, sacred principles to maintain, and rights to defend, for which we were in duty bound to do our best, even if we perished in the endeavor. * * * If it were all to be done over again, I would act in precisely the same manner."—*Lee.*

# THE SOUTH WAS RIGHT

BY

S. A. STEEL

# THE SOUTH WAS RIGHT

In 1861 eleven States of the American Union withdrew and formed themselves into the Confederate States of America. They did so under the due forms of law without revoluntionary violence, and with the most peaceable intention. The United States resolved to compel these seceded States to return into the Union by force of arms. The South resolved to defend her liberties. The war between them lasted for four years. Nearly four million men were under arms on both sides from first to last; about two thousand battles, engagements and skirmishes were fought; nearly half a million lives were lost; thousands more were maimed for life; billions of dollars' worth of property was destroyed; and no estimate can be made of the suffering inflicted on the women and children of the country, or words be found adequate to express the sorrow they endured, the loss they sustained in being deprived of educational opportunities and the means of social culture, and the universal demoralization that ensued. It was one of the most gigantic conflicts of history, and one of unparalleled bitterness. As both sides were in mortal earnest, there was no way to stop it until one of the contestants was exhausted.

After four years of heroic struggle, the South fell. To quote the language of General R. E. Lee, in his farewell address to his army at Appomattox, it was "compelled to yield to overwhelming numbers and resources." After a time the seceded States were readmitted into the Union. The people of the South, ruined by four years of strife in their territory and the destruction of their whole system of life, with all but honor lost, indulged in no idle repinings, uttered no unmanly regrets, bore with marvellous patience the horrible injustice of the "Reconstruction," made their appeal "to Time," went earnestly to work, and left their vindication to the impartial judgment of History.

Who was responsible for that awful war? As in the case of Carthage, so with the South, the victors have told the story to suit their own ends. The result is a very one-sided and misleading account. Much of what the North has written about the war is on a par with the testimony of a darky witness in court. "Mose," said the lawyer, "do you understand that you have sworn to tell the truth?" "Yas, sir." "Well, then, have you told the jury the truth about this matter?" "Yas, sir, boss, and a leetle the rise of the truth." One writer says that the North won, not because it "out-fought the South, but because it out-thought the South," that it was a victory of mind more than force. I can not agree with this. If we must keep the alliteration of the phrase, I would say that the North won, not because it could outfight the South, but because it did outwrite the South. But a vast deal of what they wrote was not true. It was pure fiction, like, for example, Whittier's poem about Barbara Fritchie, and Mrs. Stowe's Uncle Tom's Cabin. It was false, but it accomplished its purpose of hostility to the South. There are gratifying indications now that the motives of the South are beginning to be understood.

Still we frequently hear it said now that the Southerners "believed they were right." But it is nearly always said in a connection which makes it mean: Of course they were wrong, but since they believed they were right, they are entitled to the respect due to sincerity. This condescending courtesy can never satisfy honorable men. As a *modus vivendi* it may be accepted, and afford a diplomatic ground of meeting, where the sentimental "fraternity" of a superficial and emotional patriotism may disport itself in iridescent oratory. I believe in fraternity, and have tried to contribute to its establishment between the North and South; but if it must be obtained at the cost of truth, the price is too high. I have respect for the honest Northern man who was willing to lay his life on the altar of the Union, and this sentiment is perfectly consistent with a deep conviction that the South was right in the essential thing for which it fought, the right of self-government. The North has told its side: let us tell ours. We are not afraid to take the question into the high court of History.

We are not through with that struggle. Superficial people may speak and write about such matters being "in the past," and out of relation to the present; but we are dealing with conditions created by that war, issues that are still far from being settled. The man who thinks the race question is settled is incapable of understanding the subject; and that whole question grew out of the forcible emancipation of the Southern negroes. Had the South been left to handle that question in its own way, which was one of the reasons for secession, who can say that it would not be in a far more hopeful state than it is now as a result of the war? Slavery could not long have survived in the South with the sentiment of the whole outside world, and multitudes of its own people, against it. It is yet to be seen whether this government can stand, or float, with the millstone of the black race about its neck. Nor is this the only way in which the problems created by the war involve us, and are inextricably identified with present day issues. American statesmanship has never had a greater task than it has now to preserve the rights of the States, which are the bulwarks of our individual liberties, under the constant and universal pressure of the great centralized power of the Federal nation made by the war. The steady encroachment of the authority of the general government in every department, legislative, executive and judicial, especially the latter, on the functions of the States, is one of the most dangerous tendencies of our political life. And it grew directly out of the war.

I hold, therefore, that it is of the utmost importance that this generation of American youths shall have a correct knowledge of the war. I do not wish to detract from the glory of the North. And as to stirring up the passions of the past, no man in his senses thinks we must not study history because some one with a soft brain may get mad. Let the heathen rage; civilized men want the truth, the whole truth, and nothing but the truth.

To decide this question we must put ourselves back in the circumstances of the Southern people in 1860. When I say that the South was right in the great struggle with the North, I mean that it had both the legal and moral right to do what it did. I mean that under the circumstances which surrounded it, there was nothing else to do. I think General Lee expressed it exactly when he said: "We had, I was satisfied, sacred principles to maintain and rights to defend, for which we were in duty bound to do our best, even if we perished in the endeavor." General Lee never changed his mind. When it was all over, he said to General Hampton: "If it were all to do over again, I would act precisely in the same manner." A cause must be supported by some very sound reasons when such a man can speak so firmly about it. To say that the South was wrong simply because the North won, is to cast a serious reflection on the intelligence of such men as Lee, and many others. What were the reasons that made General Lee so sure that he was right when he led the Army of Northern Virginia in battles that to the end of time will be the study and the wonder of men? Well, I will give you some of them.

But first, as we are to discuss the war, let us decide on the name by which we will designate it. This is more important than some people think. As one eminently qualified to speak has reminded us, "names both record and make history." Names are not arbitrary labels, but should express or describe the nature of the thing to which they are attached. A whole philosophy may be compressed in a name, as, for example, "Idealism" or "Realism." So you see a thoughtful man can not pass lightly over the matter of a name. This is especially true of such an important subject as the one I am discussing. We must get a right name.

The North called the war "The War of the Rebellion," and gave this name to the official records of it. Now, rebellion is forcible resistance to legitimate government. But, as I hope to show, when the Southern States withdrew from the Union, the legitimate authority of the United States over them ceased, and it was not "rebellion" to resist it. This name is unfair to the

South, and it is now only used by people who have failed to outlive the prejudices of the war.

Alexander H. Stephens called it "The War Between the States," and I am sorry to see that this name has been recommended as the proper name by the Legislative Committee on the revision of the Constitution of North Carolina. This name conveys a wrong idea of the war. It was not a war between the States, but between the United States and the Confederate States, each acting as a nation. It is glaringly inaccurate and misleading.

By some it is called "The War Between the Sections." The objection to this name is that it is too vague, and gives no idea of what the war was about. It is not a name, only a label.

By some it has been called "The War of Secession." The objection to this name is that it implies that the South was responsible for the war, and this is not true. The North was the aggressor from first to last. For years before the war, it began and carried on an agitation hostile to the South, and when the South sought to protect itself by peaceable withdrawal, it invaded the South with fire and sword. That name is misleading.

The name most generally used, and which Congress has decided shall be the official name, is the "Civil War." I can not agree with Congress. A civil war is a war between two factions contending for the control of the same government, like the war between Cæsar and Pompey in Roman history, or the war between the Houses of Lancaster and York in English history. It is evident that this was not the character of our war. If the Southern States had fought in the Union it would have been a "civil war;" but they withdrew from the Union, and organized a separate government. Whether they had the right to do this does not affect the case; the fact is they did it, and that fact makes the phrase "civil war" untrue when applied to our struggle. It was a war between two nations. For the four years that it lasted, the Confederate States was a real government, possessing all the attributes and exercising all the powers of government. It was acknowledged and supported and defended by its citizens; it issued money, levied taxes, waged war, and was recognized as having belligerent rights. I can understand how this name is satisfactory to the North, for it concedes all they have claimed about the war. The plain logic of it makes it a war of "rebellion," the Southerners "rebels," Davis and Lee and Jackson "traitors," who escaped the usual fate of traitors only through the clemency of their conquerors. But I can not understand how such a name can meet the approval of intelligent Southerners. It can be justified only on the basis of Napoleon's sarcastic definition of history as "Fiction agreed upon." I never use it, and I teach my children not to use it. Its brevity may pass it with people who are in too big a hurry to tell the truth; but I have passed that point. I prefer to take a little more time and be right.

None of these names fit the facts in the case. Then what is the proper name for the war? It is this: THE WAR FOR THE UNION. That name states the truth about it. The North declared this to be the purpose of the war; it was begun, continued, and finished to preserve the Union; President Lincoln repeatedly asserted that this was the paramount issue, to which all others were subordinate; to "save the Union" he deliberately went outside of the Constitution in the exercise of arbitrary power; and if you had asked the men in blue what they were fighting for, nine out of ten of them would have said "to save the Union."

Moreover, this name expresses the result of the war; for it not only brought back into the Union the States that had gone out, but it made a new and different Union from the one we had before. It puts the responsibility, too, where it belongs, on the North—a responsibility which they are proud to accept, and which we ought to be perfectly willing to concede to them. The South acted from first to last on the defensive; the North was the aggressor. It is all now far back in the past, and the clouds of passion have floated away, so let us be brave enough to be fair and do each other the justice to admit the truth. We will never do that when we call the war "the civil war," for that indicts the whole South. Whatever Congress may say, I shall call the great struggle the War for the Union.

Perhaps there was no campaign slogan more effective in the North, no appeal to the patriotism of the country so useful, no phrases more eloquently employed than such terms as to "save the Union," to "preserve the Union," to crush "the rebellion that aims to destroy the Union." The Southern people were represented as seeking to "break up the Union." Now there was not one word of truth in such statements. Whatever we may think about the doctrine of secession as a political principle, a moment of reflection will disclose the falsity of the idea that the secession of the Southern States was an attempt to destroy the Union. Did the separation of the American Colonies from England destroy the British Empire? Did the separation of Mexico from Spain destroy the Spanish nation? Did Portugal cease to exist when Brazil withdrew to become an independent people? If the South had won in the struggle the Union would have stood just as it did before, only less in territorial extent by the area of the seceded States. The object of the South was by a peaceable separation to govern itself, and deal with its domestic problems in its own way, leaving the North to do the same. This was not to "destroy the Union." Yet this lie, booted and spurred, did valiant service against the South. However, it is only one of a multitude of "toads" which, when touched by the Ithuriel spear of truth, the cold steel of facts, spring into proper satanic shape.

The subject divides itself into two parts, first, did the Southern States have the right to secede, and second, did the circumstances justify their exercise of the right? I take the affirmative, and assert that the Southern States had the legal right to withdraw from the Union, and that the conditions under which they were compelled to act justified their withdrawal. I am willing to let history decide the question. I am not willing to accept the verdict of success. The failure of the South does not prove that it was wrong, nor does the triumph of the North prove that it was right: that only proves the North was stronger than the South. Success is no test of truth: if it is, we can justify some of the most hideous tyrannies of the past, from Tamerlane, who built his throne on the skulls of his slaughtered victims, down to the latest despot who rules by right of the sword.

Before adducing my proof of the South's legal right to withdraw from the Federal Union, let me say that the character of the Southern people furnishes a strong presumption that they had valid ground for the course they pursued. They were an intelligent people. Such men as Jefferson Davis, and Robert Tombs, and Lamar, and

Campbell, and Barnwell, and hundreds besides, were the
equals in intellectual ability, in capacity to understand
political government, and in patriotic devotion to the
principles of republican liberty, of any in the North.
I think it may be safely asserted that no people on earth
are more attached to the principles and institutions of
constitutional freedom, more jealous of their rights
under the Constitution, or more conservative in their
spirit in maintaining them, than the people of the South.
They were misrepresented to the world as a semibarba-
rous people because they had slaves.   A Federal general
told me that he was born and reared in New England,
and enlisted in one of the first regiments raised, not only
for the purpose of saving the Union, but also of liberat-
ing the slaves and subduing the "barbarians of the
South."   He said that after the war he was put in
charge of one of the Military Districts of the South,
and his official duties brought him into association with
many of the public men of the Confederacy.   He said
he was amazed to find such men.   To quote his own language, he said: "I never met a finer type of intelligent
Christian manhood in my life, and it is still a mystery
to me how you could rear such men under a system that
allowed slavery."   The Southerners were not imbeciles,
if the Ambassador to England did write them down as
such in his ridiculous book, The Southerner.   They
understood what they wanted, and their rights in the
case.   They had good ground for their conduct.   Men
like Robert E. Lee knew what they were doing, and why
they did it.   For the honor of their memory let us look
at some of their reasons. * * * * * *

# THE SOUTH WAS RIGHT.

I assert that the right of a State to withdraw from the Union is proved by the nature of the Union when it was first formed.

When the thirteen Colonies won their independence, they became sovereign States. "Virginia made a declaration on the 12th of June, 1776, renouncing her colonial dependence on Great Britain and separating herself forever from that kingdom. On the 29th of June, in the same year, she performed the highest function of independent sovereignty by adopting and ordaining a constitution prescribing an oath of fealty and allegiance for all who might hold office under her authority, and that remained as the organic law of the Old Dominion until 1829."

All the other Colonies became sovereign States in the same way. These independent States sent delegates to a Convention which made a Declaration of Independence. This Declaration affirmed that they were "free and independent States." When the War of the Revolution closed, they were recognized by England as "free, sovereign, and independent States." The loose confederation which had been formed at first, and which was held together only by the necessity of united action in the common struggle for freedom, being found inadequate for the purposes of a Federal government, a new Union was formed by the adoption of a Constitution. The right of secession was implicit in this document.

In 1830 Webster made a celebrated speech in reply to Hayne of South Carolina. This was an epochal speech, and, perhaps, did more than anything else to promote and establish the Northern idea of the Union, for it became a school classic. Millions of school boys declaimed it, and were educated in their political opinions by it. So far as the speech was a reply to Hayne's doctrine of Nullification, I think Webster demolished him. That doctrine held that a State could declare a law passed by Congress null and void in its bounds. I do not think such a doctrine can be derived from the Constitution, or be harmonized with its principles. But Webster was clearly in error when he claimed in that speech that the Constitution "emanated immediately from the people." Webster misconstrued the words, "We, the people," in the preamble to the Constitution. On the strength of these words he held that the Federal government was "a popular government," "erected by the people."

That is true, but not in the sense in which Webster meant it, for he meant, as he said, that it "emanated immediately from the people." It did not emanate immediately from the people, but mediately from the people, acting through the States. Now, if this is true, the whole premise of Webster's famous argument is false, and the immense conclusions based on it must go by the board. This is a daring assertion in view of Webster's great fame; but it is true, nevertheless. Look at the facts in the case. When it was decided to create a new and stronger Union, Congress *recommended*— mark that word—to the States that they send delegates to a convention, which should "revise the Articles of Confederation, and report to Congress *and the several legislatures* (italics mine) such alterations and provisions therein as shall, when agreed to in Congress *and confirmed by the States*, render the Federal Constitution adequate to the exigencies of government and the preservation of the Union." The States, as States, took action on this recommendation. A majority of the

States accepted it, and appointed delegates to the Convention that framed the Constitution. When this Constitution was finished, it was submitted, not to the people *en masse*, but to the several *States* for their adoption. Their ratification was necessary to give it validity and force. The *States* called conventions to consider whether they should adopt it. A majority ratified it, but Virginia and New York did so only after long and earnest debate, and not until a long time after the others had acted. North Carolina and Rhode Island held out still longer; and Virginia accepted the Constitution only on the condition that certain amendments should be added to it. Professor John Fiske makes it as clear as the sun at noon, in his book, "The Critical Period of American History," that the *States* were the parties to the Federal compact, and that without their concurrence there could have been no Union. From all this, and much more that might be adduced, I am bound to think that Webster's famous postulate that the Constitution "emanated immediately from the people" will not stand the test of facts. History disproves it. The Federal Union was created by the American people acting in their capacity as sovereign States. With all due respect to the memory of Webster, I do not see how any other conclusion can be reached from the facts.

But that you may not think this the conclusion of a layman, I will reinforce it with the confirmation of two minds worthy to rank with Webster himself as political statesmen. No man who had a hand in making the Constitution was more capable of understanding it than Madison. He was there when the Constitution was under discussion and was familiar with the purpose and spirit of the convention that made it. He derived his knowledge not from historical records and tradition, as Webster did, but from actual contact with the work and personal experience in framing the immortal document. Madison said: "The assent and ratification of the people, not as individuals composing an entire nation, but as composing distinct and independent States to which they belong, are the sources of the Constitution. It is, therefore, not a national, but a federal compact." That flatly contradicts Webster's doctrine that the Constitution "emanated immediately from the people." The other authority I quote is the Hon. J. L. M. Curry, one of the ablest of our Southern statesmen. He said: "It (the Constitution) was transmitted to the several State Legislatures, to be by them submitted to State conventions, and each State for itself ratified at different times, without concert of action, except in the result to be ascertained. As the jurisdiction of a State was limited to its own territory, its ratification was limited to its own people. The Constitution got its validity, its vitality, not from the inhabitants as constituting one great nation, nor from the people of all the States considered as one people, but from the concurrent action of a prescribed number of States, each acting separately and pretending to no claim or right to act for or control other States. That each of these States had the right to decline to ratify and remain out of the Union for all time to come, no sane man will deny." Dr. Curry had access to the same sources of information as Webster, was as capable of understanding the matter, and was as loyal to the Constitution; yet he reached a conclusion the very opposite of Webster's. His conclusion has the great advantage over Webster, too, in that Curry refers to the facts in support of his view, while Webster simply made the bold assertion without proof. Webster was wrong. The States made the Union.

Furthermore, the States not only created the Union, but the record shows that in ratifying the Constitution, and forming the Union, they did not extinguish their own sovereignty, but on the contrary, definitely reserved to themselves all the powers not expressly delegated to the general government; and in particular *the right to withdraw from the Union*. Look at the facts. When Virginia ratified the Constitution, and thus entered the Union, she said: "The delegates do, in the name and in behalf of the people of Virginia, declare and make known that the powers granted under the Constitution, being derived from the people of the United States, *may be resumed* by them whensoever the same shall be perverted to their injury or oppression, and that every power not granted thereby remains with them at their will." There is no ambiguity in that language. It shows how Virginia understood her relation to the Union, and it is important to keep it in mind; for it was on this very ground that Virginia acted when she seceded from the Union. She simply did in 1861 what she reserved the right to do in 1788.

When New York ratified the Constitution, and entered the Union, she made it even more emphatic that she understood that if the Union was not true to its purpose she could withdraw. Her people said: "The powers of government may be resumed by the people whenever it should become necessary to their happiness, that every power, jurisdiction, and right which is not by the said Constitution clearly delegated to the Congress of the United States or the departments of the government thereof, remains to the people of the several States, or to their respective State governments, to whom they may have granted the same."

What Virginia and New York did all the rest did. The Union was, therefore, based upon the mutual consent of independent States, not to surrender absolutely, but to delegate to the Union certain attributes of sovereignty that were necessary to the general government. The supreme attribute of sovereignty they unquestionably reserved, which was the right to recall the powers granted to the general government. We are not now discussing the merits of the doctrine of secession; we are simply looking the fact squarely in the face, and I do not see how any one can doubt, much less deny, that the right inhered in the compact as one of its fundamental principles, and was so understood by all the parties. In view of the mutual jealousies that prevailed at that time between the States composing the Union, it is as certain as anything of the kind can be that if any State had supposed it could not withdraw from the Union, it never would have entered it. Those who formed the Union were not blind to the danger this kind of association involved; but no other sort of Union was possible then, and this Union was all that was needed as long as the States were faithful to the Constitution. The great men who built our wonderful Union trusted to the patriotism of the people to obey the Constitution as the supreme law. And if the North had not violated the Constitution, the South never would have invoked the legal right of secession to protect herself against oppression. But the right was there.

I think I have established my first point, namely, that the right of a State to withdraw from the Union is proved by the nature of the Union when it was first formed. I will now advance to my second argument.

The right of the State to withdraw from the Union is proved by the fact that this doctrine was held by all parts of the country for a long period after the Union was formed.

The fact that the South adhered to this original understanding of the Union, and when its rights were threatened, actually appealed to it for protection, has led many to think that the doctrine of secession was a Southern theory. But the truth is that it was not only held equally in the North, but New England was the first to threaten to put it in use. She did not do so, not because she doubted the right, but because her interests fortunately did not demand it. It is, perhaps, hardly admissible to cite the testimony of Southern men on this point; nobody in the South doubted the right of a State to secede. So I will restrict myself to the testimony of Northern men.

In 1811 a bill was before Congress to admit Louisiana into the Union. New England bitterly opposed the bill. Josiah Quincy, member of Congress from Massachusetts, made a speech in opposition to the measure. In this speech he said: "If this bill passes, the bonds of the Union are virtually dissolved. The States which compose it are free from their moral obligation. *And as it is the right of all* (italics mine), so it will be the duty of some to prepare for separation, amicably if they can, forcibly if they must." Here we have one of the foremost statesmen of New England asserting on the floor of Congress that secession is a right of all the States; and nobody seems to have contradicted him. Nobody could contradict him, for at that time everybody admitted the right.

[ 23 ]

## THE SOUTH WAS RIGHT.

In 1828, only two years before his famous speech promulgating the new doctrine of an "indissoluble Union," Webster prosecuted Theodore Lyman, of Boston, for libel. Lyman had charged that Webster was guilty of treasonable conduct because he had taken part in a plot to dissolve the Union which was begun in New England in 1807. Lyman was defended by Samuel Hubbard, who afterward became a Justice of the Supreme Court of Massachusetts. Hubbard held that the charge was not libellous, because "a confederation of New England States to confer with each other on the subject of dissolving the Union was not treason. The several States are independent, and not dependent. Every State has the right to secede from the Union." Here we have a distinct assertion of the right of secession by an eminent New England jurist.

William Rawle was one of the most eminent legal authorities in his day. He was for many years Chancellor of the Law Association of Philadelphia, and the author of The Revised Code of Pennsylvania. He was the author of a book called "Views of the Constitution," which is said to have been a textbook in the West Point Military Academy when many of the men who adhered to the South in the separation were students there. This, of course, gave the doctrines of the book the official endorsement of the government. Here is what Rawle said about the Union: "The Union was formed by the voluntary agreement of the States, and in uniting together they have not forfeited their nationality, nor have they been reduced to one and the same people. If one of the States chooses to withdraw its name from the contract, it would be difficult to disprove its right of doing so; and the Federal government would have no

means of maintaining its claim, either by force or right.
* * * It depends on the State itself to retain or abolish
the principle of representation, because it depends on
itself whether it will continue a member of the Union.
* * * To deny this right would be inconsistent with the
principles on which our political systems are founded.
The right must be considered an original ingredient in
the composition of the general government, which,
though not expressed, was mutually understood. * * *
The secession of a State from the Union depends on the
will of the people of such State."

Let me remind you that I am not advocating the
doctrine of secession. These clear and strong testimonies may unconsciously bias you to that thought.
The doctrine was shot to death on a thousand bloody
battlefields, and there is no resurrection for it. What
I am doing is to prove to the young people of today
that the people of the South in 1861 had the legal right
to secede. And I think the testimony of these Northern
men, men who rank among their foremost for ability,
virtue and patriotism, demonstrate beyond a doubt that
the people of the North held the doctrine as well as those
of the South. How could that be "rebellion" and
"treason" in 1860 which was taught, with the sanction
of the government, twenty years before in the very
school which of all others needed to inculcate correct
ideas of duty? Yet what the government taught was
truth in 1840 was declared to be rank "rebellion" in
1860! But let me quote some more testimony on this
point, the original right of a State to secede, for it is
very interesting to see how the logic of facts compels
even the most reluctant to admit it. Truth is mighty
and will prevail. The satanic proverb may be true,

that a lie can get around the world while truth is pulling on its boots; but, however slow-footed truth may be, it overtakes the lie in the end. Truth has a marvelous staying power. "The eternal years of God are hers." Did not Gen. Sherman say something about "the revenges of history?" Well, they are very real.

In 1860 the South had no more vigorous hater than Goldwin Smith. His pen did valiant service for the North, and hindered abroad that recognition of the Confederate States by foreign powers, which was the only chance of success the South had. Yet thirty years after the war, when his passion had subsided, when the Falsehood he had defended stood forth, stripped by impartial Time of its disguise, he said of Secession: "Few who have looked into history can doubt that the Union originally was a compact, dissoluble, perhaps, most of them would have said, at pleasure; dissoluble certainly on breach of the articles of Union." It must be very strong evidence to compel that admission from such an opponent. Of course it is charitable to think that when he was denouncing us in 1860-65 as "rebels," "traitors" and semibarbarians, and clamoring for our extermination, pleading with England to hands off and let Uncle Sam wipe us from the earth—I say it is charitable to think that when he was doing this he had not "looked into history." It was the audacity of ignorance.

Hon. Henry Cabot Lodge, who is a senator from Massachusetts, wrote the life of Webster in the American Statesmen Series. In that work Lodge says: "When the Constitution was adopted by the votes of States at Philadelphia, and accepted by the votes of States in popular conventions, it is safe to say that there was not a man in the country, from Washington and Hamilton, on the one side, to George Clinton and George Mason, on the other, who regarded the new system as anything but an experiment entered upon by the States, and from which each and every State had the right peaceably to withdraw, a right which was very likely to be exercised."

I will quote only one more testimony, but that is from a man who, though he fought against us, is fair and open-minded, and whose manly and honest utterances about the South and her great struggle have helped to clear the clouds of prejudice from the skies. I mean Gen. Charles Francis Adams, President of the Massachusetts Historical Society. In his noble address on the occasion of the Lee Centennial at Washington and Lee University, an address noble for its manly frankness and fraternal spirit, Gen. Adams said this:

"The technical argument—the logic of the proposition—seems plain, and, to my thought, unanswerable. The original sovereignty was indisputably in the State; in order to establish a nationality certain attributes of sovereignty were ceded by the States to a common central organization; all attributes not thus specifically conceded were reserved to the States, and no attributes of moment were to be construed as conceded by implication. There is no attribute of sovereignty so important as allegiance—citizenship. So far all is elementary. Now we come to the crux of the proposition. Not only was allegiance—the right to define and establish citizenship—not among the attributes specifically conceded by the several States to the central nationality, but, on the contrary, it was explicitly reserved, the instrument declaring that 'the citizens of each State should be entitled to all the privileges and immunities of citizens in the several States.' *Ultimate allegiance was, therefore, due to the State which defined and created citizenship, and not to the central organization which accepted as citizens whomever the States pronounced to be such."* (Italics mine.)

This testimony is all the stronger in that Adams takes the other side of the question as to the right of secession. Let us admit that there are two sides to the subject. It is preposterous to suppose the North did not have some ground on which to stand. But so did the South, and as far as I have been able to see, the immense preponderance of proof is on the Southern side. I think I have established my second point, namely, that the right of a State to secede from the Union was the understanding of all parts of the country for a long period after the Union was formed. I will now advance to my third argument.

The right of a State to withdraw from the Union, or at least the fact of secession, and, by implication, the grounds on which it was exercised, is proved by the treatment of the seceded States after the war. Here again let us face the facts.

Eleven States, acting on their constitutional right, as they claimed, by due and proper process of law, reassumed the powers they had originally ceded to the Federal Union, and became what they were in the beginning, free, sovereign, and independent States. The North denied the right of these States to withdraw, and held that a State once in the Union was in forever. This was the view Mr. Lincoln held, and on which he proceeded to act. According to this view the Confederates were a lawless combination of disaffected people within the

States that claimed to have seceded, in rebellion against the legitimate authority of the Federal government, which the President was in duty bound to suppress. It was to maintain the doctrine that a State could not secede from the Union that the North fought the war to a finish. The emancipation of the slaves of the South was definitely proclaimed as a war measure, and justified on the ground that it was necessary to preserve the Union.

Now on this theory, it was self-evident that when the lawless combinations in rebellion against the government in the seceded States were overcome, and the Federal authority acknowledged by all, the States were in their former relation to the Union. That had never been changed, for, they said, a State in once is in forever. Gen. Sherman and Gen. Johnston made their agreement for the surrender of Johnston's army on the basis of this theory, an agreement which was promptly rejected by the authorities at Washington, ostensibly on the ground that military commanders in the field could not meddle with political matters; but they really had other things in mind.

This is the place for a good story of Johnston's surrender, told by John S. Wise in his entertaining book, "The End of An Era." It is a little long, but will put a little spice in the otherwise dry argument. Wise says: "Johnston had known Sherman well in the United States army. Their first interview near Greensboro resulted in an engagement to meet for further discussion the following day. As they were parting, Johnston remarked: 'By the way, Cumps, Breckenridge, our Secretary of War, is with me. He is a very able fellow, and a better lawyer than any of us. If there is no objection, I will fetch him along tomorrow.'

"Bristling up, General Sherman exclaimed, 'Secretary of War! No, no; we don't recognize any civil government among you fellows, Joe. No, I don't want any Secretary of War.'

" 'Well,' said General Johnston, 'he is also a major general in the Confederate army. Is there any objection to his presence in the capacity of major general?'

" 'Oh!' quoth Sherman, in his characteristic way, 'major general! Well, any major general you may bring I shall be glad to meet. But recollect, Johnston, no Secretary of War. Do you understand?'

"The next day General Johnston, accompanied by Major General Breckenridge, was at the rendezvous before Sherman.

" 'You know how fond of his liquor Breckenridge was?' added General Johnston, as he went on with his story. 'Well, nearly everything to drink had been absorbed. For several days Breckenridge had found it difficult, if not impossible, to procure liquor. He showed the effect of his enforced abstinence. He was rather dull and heavy that morning. Somebody in Danville had given him a plug of very fine chewing tobacco, and he chewed vigorously while we were awaiting Sherman's coming. After awhile the latter arrived. He bustled in with a pair of saddlebags over his arm, and apologized for being late. He placed his saddlebags carefully upon a chair. Introductions followed, and for a while General Sherman made himself exceedingly agreeable. Finally, some one suggested that we had better take up the matter in hand.'

" 'Yes,' said Sherman; 'but, gentlemen, it occurred to me that perhaps you were not overstocked with liquor, and I procured some medical stores on my way over. Will you join me before we begin work?'

"General Johnston said he watched the expression of Breckenridge at this announcement, and it was beatific. Tossing his quid into the fire, he rinsed his mouth, and when the bottle and the glass were passed to him he poured out a tremendous drink, which he swallowed with great satisfaction. With an air of content, he stroked his mustache and took a fresh chew of tobacco. Then they settled down to business, and Breckenridge never shone more brilliantly than he did in the discussion which followed. He seemed to have at his tongue's end every rule and maxim of international and constitutional law, and of the laws of war—international wars, civil wars, and wars of rebellion. In fact, he was so resourceful, cogent, persuasive, learned, that, at one stage of the proceedings, General Sherman, when confronted by the authority, but not convinced by the eloquence or learning of Breckenridge, pushed back his chair, and exclaimed: 'See here, gentlemen, who is doing this surrendering anyhow? If this thing goes on, you'll have me sending a letter of apology to Jeff Davis.'

"Afterward, when they were nearing the close of the conference, Sherman sat for some time absorbed in deep thought. Then he arose, went to the saddlebags and fumbled for the bottle. Breckenridge saw the movement. Again he took his quid from his mouth and tossed it into the fireplace. His eye brightened, and he gave every evidence of intense interest in what Sherman seemed about to do. The latter, preoccupied, perhaps unconscious of his action, poured out some liquor,

[ 31 ]

shoved the bottle back into the saddle-pocket, walked to the window and stood there, looking out abstractedly, while he sipped his grog. From pleasant hope and expectation the expression on Breckenridge's face changed successively to uncertainty, disgust and deep depression. At last his hand sought the plug of tobacco, and, with an injured, sorrowful look, he cut off another chew. Upon this he ruminated during the remainder of the interview, taking little part in what was said.

"After silent reflections at the window, General Sherman bustled back, gathered up his papers, and said: 'These terms are too generous, but I must hurry away before you make me sign a capitulation. I will submit them to the authorities at Washington, and let you hear how they are received.' With that he bade the assembled officers adieu, took his saddlebags on his arm and went off as he had come.

"General Johnston took occasion, as they left the house and were drawing on their gloves, to ask General Breckenridge how he had been impressed by Sherman.

"'Sherman is a bright man, and a man of great force,' replied Breckenridge, speaking with deliberation, 'but,' raising his voice and with a look of great intensity, 'General Johnston, General Sherman is a hog. Yes, sir, a *hog*. Did you see him take that drink by himself?'

"General Johnston tried to assure General Breckenridge that General Sherman was a royal good fellow, but the most absent-minded man in the world. He told him that the failure to offer him a drink was the highest compliment that could have been paid to the masterly arguments with which he had pressed the Union commander to that state of abstraction.

[ 32 ]

# THE SOUTH WAS RIGHT.

"'Ah!' protested the big Kentuckian, half sighing, half grieving, 'no Kentucky gentleman would ever have taken away that bottle. He knew we needed it, and needed it badly.'

"The story was well told, and I did not make it public until after General Johnston's death. On one occasion, being intimate with General Sherman, I repeated it to him. Laughing heartily, he said: 'I don't remember it, but if Joe Johnston told it, it was so. Those fellows hustled me so that day I was sorry for the drink I did give them,' and with that sally he broke into fresh laughter."

The story is a fine illustration of the force of the Confederate argument. Breckenridge, doubtless, shrewdly accepted Sherman's theory of the relation of Confederates to the Union, and on that ground but one conclusion could be logically reached. Sherman had told Johnston "we don't recognize any civil government among you fellows," and refused to consent to the presence of Breckenridge in his character of Secretary of War of the Confederate States. According to Sherman's theory, which was the theory of the Federal government from the beginning of the struggle, no State had left the Union, or could leave the Union. Of course, on this theory, the States, as States, were in exactly the same relation to the Union as they were before the trouble began. So, when the armed resistance to Federal authority within their borders ceased, they would logically, and naturally, and automatically, resume their rights and exercise their powers. No wonder Sherman was "abstracted" as he sat in the window. He was right; the truth about their high-handed and unlawful conduct demanded "an apology to Jeff Davis" and the civilized world. Sherman's sword was irresistible; but when the case came into court, the truth was all-powerful, and made the victor "absent minded."

But the government at Washington did not intend to allow the Confederate Secretary of War to win a brilliant diplomatic victory. Their argument from the first had been the sword, the argument of superior force. They had won the case with that argument. The South was defeated, exhausted, prostrate, and at their mercy. They did not intend to allow it to get upon its feet. Revenge and punishment were in order next.

So they deliberately reversed the theory on which they had fought the war to a victorious end, and after spending billions of money and sacrificing hundreds of thousands of lives to uphold the doctrine that a State once in the Union was in forever, they declared that the seceded States were out of the Union and proceeded to readmit them into the Union. I am not now concerned with the inconsistency of this course; but I hold that, whatever may have been its motive, its wisdom or unwisdom, it completely admits the paramount position of the South—that a State could withdraw from the Union. I think I have established my third point—namely, that the treatment of the seceded States after the war proved that a State could withdraw from the Union. I will now advance to my fourth argument.

The right of a State to withdraw from the Union is proved by the failure of the government to try Jefferson Davis, or any other Confederate officer, when the war was over. I admit that this argument is an inferential one; but the facts are so significant that they are of great force in the case.

## THE SOUTH WAS RIGHT.

According to the theory of the government from the beginning to the close of the war, Davis and all other Confederates were traitors and were liable to all the consequences of treason. During the war they were uniformly accused by the North of treason, called "rebels" and the war a "rebellion," and public opinion clamored for their punishment as "traitors." When Davis and other Confederates were captured they were thrown into prison and treated as if they were in fact traitors. One by one they were released without trial. Davis was formally indicted, but was not brought to trial. He earnestly desired it, so did his friends, and the whole South, confident that he would not only be acquitted of treason, but that the result of the trial would demonstrate to the whole civilized world the legal justice of the Southern cause. After a long imprisonment, Davis was released on bail, and the case against him was finally dismissed.

Why was Davis and the rest of the Confederates never tried for the crime with which they were accused with such unanimity and vehemence during the war? It cannot be ascribed to magnanimity on the part of the conquerors. I wish I could think it was, for it would help to clear away one of the darkest blots on the fair name of American civilization. But the facts forbid the idea. The largest magnanimity of thought about it now, when all motive for unjust accusation has vanished in the kinder spirit that prevails, is unable to reconcile the treatment of Mr. Davis as a prisoner in Fortress Monroe with the idea of magnanimity. He was held in rigorous confinement, compelled to be under a bright light and the sleepless eye of a guard night and day: his health was broken and wasted with four years of

[ 35 ]

anxiety and care; yet they put handcuffs on his wrists and ball and chain on his ankles, not for security, but to degrade and humiliate him and the South; they refused him all intercourse with his family and friends; when his little three-year-old girl asked "if she might write to papa," they consented, provided what she wrote was proper for him to read. Instructed by her devoted mother, and to be sure that what she wrote would not be refused, knowing that just the sight of her handwriting would comfort her afflicted father, the little girl copied the twenty-third Psalm, but they refused to allow it to go to him. Oh, no! In the dark souls of the men who were in power then there was no thought of clemency, and they were as incapable of magnanimity as the Prior of the Spanish Inquisition. They tortured Davis with a refinement of cruelty that will damn their memory forever, and which no effervescence of patriotic twentieth century fraternity can expunge.

Why did they not try him? They had everything their way except one thing, and they were afraid of that, and that was *truth*. The Sword could slaughter its thousands. The Torch could reduce to ashes the sacred homes and shrines of the South. A million men in arms, the seasoned veterans of a hundred battles, could make the nations stand in awe. But the Sword and the Torch and the Bayonets of a million men recoiled from the adamantine front of Truth as it was represented in the frail, emaciated person of Jefferson Davis. They could persecute him, but they were afraid to prosecute him. Justice held her shield above him and they left him. Davis had eminent counsel, among them Daniel O'Connell, the famous Irish barrister, and his trial would have been one of international interest. Secure in the power of

the Sword, the victors were too wise to allow their title
to be tested by the law before a court of justice. The
trial of Jefferson Davis would have afforded the South
a splendid opportunity to vindicate itself before the
civilized world, and I have not a shadow of doubt that it
would have settled the whole responsibility for the war
where it belonged, on the North, and proved beyond dispute that they, and not the Southerners, were in
"rebellion" against the Constitution on which the Union
was founded in the beginning.

But enough has been said to show that the States up
to 1860 had a legal right to withdraw from the Union.
That right no longer exists, but it did exist then; and it
was the definite ground on which the Southern people
acted. The fallacies of the Northern argument against
it are easily exposed. For example: It was said that
as the Constitution itself was silent on the question of
secession, it was a matter of construction, and the North
had as much right to construe it against secession as the
South had to construe it in favor of it. The answer to
that is that it is a principle universally admitted that a
document must be construed according to the intention
of those who made it. I have shown in the evidence I
have given that those who made the Union understood
that the States had the right to withdraw from it. When
the North, therefore, construed the Constitution to
forbid secession, they did so in violation of the universal
rule of interpretation of legal documents. The South in
this respect had the right on its side.

Again: In his first inaugural address, Mr. Lincoln
said: "If the United States be not a government proper,
but an association of States in the nature of a contract
merely, can it, as a contract, be peaceably unmade by less

than all the parties who made it?  One party to a contract may violate it—break it, so to speak—but does it not require all to lawfully rescind it?"

It is strange that so clear a reasoner as Mr. Lincoln undoubtedly was, did not see that the simple and unanswerable reply to that is that it depends on the nature of the contract.  If when the contract was made it was understood by all the parties to the transaction that each one had the right to withdraw from the contract, and if this right was expressly reserved, then a notice of withdrawal was a legal dissolution of the compact.  Now I have shown that all the parties to this Union did understand when it was first formed that they had the right to withdraw, and several of them expressly reserved that right.  It did not, therefore, "require all to lawfully rescind it."  Notice of withdrawal was a legal dissolution.

Again: It was said that the founders of the Union intended it to be perpetual.  Mr. Lincoln stressed that point.  He said: "I hold that in contemplation of universal law, and of the Constitution, the Union of these States is perpetual.  Perpetuity is implied, if not expressed, in the fundamental law of all national governments."  Most assuredly.  But there is a difference between a "national government" and a *Federal* government, such as was in the "contemplation" of the framers of our Union in the beginning.  In a federal union perpetuity depends on the fidelity of all parties to the contract.  I take it that no sane man will claim that a national government, such as Lincoln had in mind, and which he succeeded in establishing, would have met with any favor with the founders of the American Union.  Hamilton, perhaps, dreamed of it and desired it, but the solidarity and centralized authority which it involved too nearly resembled the monarchical power they were throwing off for them to favor it. They intended it to be perpetual only on the condition that they all obeyed the Constitution; if that fundamental law of the Union was disregarded and broken they were absolved and had the legal right to withdraw. The idea of unconditional perpetuity was read into the Constitution by the North long after the Union was formed.

The true history of the Union seems to be as follows: After the American colonies had won their independence from Great Britain, they became sovereign States. For the more effective purposes of government these States, in their capacity as sovereign States, formed a *federal* union, and adopted a Constitution. This Union was intended to be perpetual, but only upon the condition of the faithful observance of the fundamental law of the Constitution. They all understood that they had the reserved right to withdraw from the Union if the Constitution was not obeyed. Gradually the idea of a *national*, instead of a *federal*, compact grew up in the North. The economic development of the Northern States favored this idea. The great influx of European emigration introduced into the North a multitude of people who knew nothing of State Rights—had no sympathy with the South, were violently opposed to African slavery, and to whom the very name of the Union was the synonym of the liberty they craved, and came to America to enjoy. This idea of a National Union, one and indissoluble forever, found an eloquent spokesman in Danial Webster, and spread like wildfire from New England to California. A whole generation in the North was reared up to believe that the Union was created immediately by the people, and that it was supreme over the States, and that loyalty to the Union was the first duty of all Americans. On the other hand, the South adhered to the idea that the Union was not national, but federal, in its nature; that it was made by the States, and had strictly limited powers; and that if the Constitution was violated every State had the right to withdraw from the Union. The economic interests of the South as an agricultural country favored this theory. Generation after generation of Southerners from the beginning were reared, and lived, and died in this political faith. And they gave it up only when they fell bleeding at every pore. This was the difference between the North and the South in 1860.

What part did slavery have in it? A very great part. The poor African savages were run down in their native jungles by cruel English and American slave-hunters and brought to this country in New England ships by Yankee slave dealers. They were bought and sold in Boston as well as in Charleston. But their labor proved unprofitable in the rigorous climate and on the sterile soil of New England, while it was highly profitable in the South. So the shrewd New Englanders unloaded the few slaves they had for good money on the South. They then became very virtuous and discovered that slavery was a horrible crime, and demanded that the South should liberate the slaves. As the North did not have slaves and the South did this became a *sectional* issue. It was the North against the South. So they grew apart both in their political convictions and in their property interests. This went on until the dispute culminated in the terrible war for the Union.

Let me resort to a parable to illustrate the relation of the Negro to the struggle. Once there were two men who were neighbors. They were very friendly for a long time, but gradually they became estranged. Mr. Smith had a large black dog. He was worthless to him and Smith was anxious to get rid of him. Finding that his neighbor, Jones, wanted a dog he sold him his black Newfoundland. The dog soon became very useful to Jones. He trained him to go errands and bring or carry packages, and in various ways to render service. The dog was well treated, indeed, he was one of the family, and a strong attachment existed between him and all the household. This excited the envy of Mr. Smith, who was an editor, and he began to write cruel things in his paper about people who made their dogs work. Jones was a high-spirited man, and he resented the unjust things Smith said. This only made Smith worse. One day he came over to Jones' home and said: "Jones, you have got to let that dog go. You shan't make him work for you any longer." Jones told Smith that it was none of his business: the law protected him in his right to the dog, and he could leave. Smith said he did not care what the law said; there was "a higher law," and he intended to see that that dog was turned loose. All this passed on the front door step. When Smith attempted to enter the house, Jones hit him straight between the eyes. Then the fight began. Smith got the worst of it for awhile, but he went away and hired a German, an Irishman, a Bohemian and a Negro, and with these to help him, he forced his way into Jones' house. All the furniture was smashed in the struggle. Jones' wife and children were driven out, and the place was wrecked. But they held their ground manfully, the faithful dog helping Jones all he could. "Fire the barn," shouted Smith, and the Irishman hurled the torch to the barn.

## THE SOUTH WAS RIGHT.

"Burn the house," shouted Smith, and the German set fire to the home. Then all of them fell upon Jones, who, exhausted by the unequal and long protracted contest, sank under the overwhelming odds. All five of them sat on poor Jones, and the big Negro put his foot on Jones' neck and spit in his face. When they had gratified their anger they made him promise before they would let him up that he would not make the dog do any more work. Then they left him.

In this parable Smith represents the North, Jones represents the South, and the dog represents the Negro. Jones fought, not to keep the dog, but to defend his rights as a man and a free citizen against the impudent and lawless intrusion of Smith into his private affairs. The North demanded that the South set the Negroes free. The South told the North to attend to her own business. Then the North resolved to force the South to yield to her demand, and the South fought to a finish for her rights. Of course, there should have been no fight, for fighting is a barbarous method of settling difficulties; but who was to blame, Jones or Smith? A man who won't defend his home against the unwarranted intermeddling of outsiders is a cowardly wretch who deserves to be kicked out of any decent community. I think Jones did exactly right. * * * * * *

Having shown that the States up to 1860 had the right to withdraw from the Union, I now take up the second part of the subject. Admitting they had the right, did the circumstances justify them in exercising it? Here again I unhesitatingly take the affirmative and appeal to the facts.

In 1860 very few people in the South doubted the legal right of a State to secede from the Union; but a great many doubted the wisdom of it and earnestly advised against it. Jefferson Davis held that a State could secede, but he opposed resorting to this extreme measure. Mr. Davis was as much misunderstood in the North as Mr. Lincoln was in the South. He earnestly deprecated an armed conflict with the North, yet he was under no delusion either as to its certainty in case of secession, or as to its character. In her interesting book, "A Diary from Dixie," Mrs. Chesnut relates a conversation with Mr. Davis just before the battle of First Manassas, or Bull Run, as we called it. She says: "In Mrs. Davis' drawing-room last night the President took a seat by me on a sofa where I sat. He talked for nearly an hour. He laughed at our faith in our own powers. We are like the British. We think every Southerner equal to three Yankees at least. We will have to be equivalent to a dozen now. After his experience of the fighting qualities of Southerners in Mexico he believes that we will do all that can be done by pluck and muscle, endurance and dogged courage, dash and red-hot patriotism. And yet his tone was not sanguine. There was a sad refrain running through it all. For one thing, either way, he thinks it will be a long war. That floored me at once. It had been too long for me already. Then he said, before the end came we would have many a bitter experience. He said only fools doubted the courage of the Yankees or their willingness to fight when they saw fit. And now that we have stung their pride we have roused them till they will fight like devils." I think that puts Mr. Davis in a new light to some people. Instead of being the rabid fire-eater and over-confident revolutionary leader many have supposed that he was, he appears to have taken a very sober and sensible view of the situation, to have fully appreciated the character of the Northern people and to realize the true nature of the struggle on which the South had entered.

General R. E. Lee was opposed to secession. He did not believe in it as a remedy for our wrongs, and said "secession is nothing but revolution." But we must always remember, when we say General Lee did not believe in secession, that he did not mean he did not believe the State had the right to secede. His conduct proved that he did believe it, and he said so. He said: "The act of Virginia in withdrawing herself from the Union carried him along as a citizen of Virginia, and her laws and acts were binding on him. I and my people considered the act of the State legitimate, and that the seceding States were merely using their reserved rights, which they had a legal right to do." So firmly convinced was General Lee of the justice of the Southern cause that he did not consider the consequences of the struggle. Succeed or fail, duty demanded that we defend our rights. He said: "We had, I was satisfied, sacred principles to maintain and rights to defend, for which we were in duty bound to do our best, even if we perished in the endeavor." This was said on the eve of Appomattox, when the ruin of the cause was unmistakable, and said by a man who never spoke at random. After the war, when he had time to review it all and the leisure and calm needful for safe conclusions, he said: "I fought against the people of the North because I believed they were seeking to wrest from the people of the South their dearest rights." He said to General Hampton: "If it were all to do over again, I would act in precisely the same manner." That does not sound like he ever had any doubts about the righteousness of the cause. Yet General Lee, after the war, testified before the Committee on Reconstruction as follows: "I may have said and I may have believed that the position of the two sections which they held to each other was brought about by the politicians of the country; that the great masses of the people, if they had understood the real question, would have avoided it. * * * I did believe at the time that it was an unnecessary condition of affairs and might have been avoided, if forbearance and wisdom had been practiced on both sides." It would be hard to frame a more truthful statement of the case.

But not only was the wisdom of secession doubted among the prominent leaders, many among the rank and file of the people doubted it. We lived in Mississippi and my father was a private citizen and a Methodist minister. He believed the State had the right to secede, but he regarded the secession movement as little short of political madness. He clung to the Union and earnestly opposed secession. He continued to oppose it long after Mississippi had seceded, and with such earnestness that our neighbors were offended, and some would not hear him preach. But when Lincoln called for troops to invade the South he exclaimed: "That ends it. If he can do that he can do anything." So, like all the rest, he was forced to take sides, and with us there was but one side to take.

Two paramount considerations controlled the South in taking the step of secession. First, the growing hostility of the North to the South, and, second, the attitude of the North toward the Constitution. Let us look at these reasons. First, the hostility of the North. The hostility of the North is seen in three things: First, opposition to the territorial expansion of the South;

second, its persistent attack on the local institutions of the South, and, third, continued misrepresentation and defamation of the people of the South.

First, the North was hostile to the territorial expansion of the South. There was no particular or strenuous opposition to "the Louisiana Purchase" under Jefferson's administration, because the two sections were still friendly, and the mutual jealousy had hardly had time to begin its evil work. But it soon began to show itself, and as we have seen, Josiah Quincy declared the admission of Louisiana would be a just cause for the dissolution of the Union. It wrought immense mischief when the boundary of the Louisiana Purchase was settled. The American minister in Madrid had secured the consent of Spain to recognize the Rio Grande as the southern boundary instead of the Sabine River. This alarmed New England. Such an immense expansion of Southern territory would never do. To prevent it, President Adams had the negotiations transferred from Madrid to Washington. Once there, it was easy to hint to the Spanish minister that if he would contend for it he could make the Sabine the line. He was not slow to take the hint. So New England statesmanship, through hostility to Southern expansion, deliberately gave back Texas to Spain. When Andrew Jackson discovered the facts, he went to work to recover what would have been ours but for the opposition of New England. He sent Houston to Texas to foment a revolt from Mexico. When Texas, after winning her independence, sought admission into the Union, New England earnestly opposed it. It succeeded only by the skin of the teeth, and through Jackson's vigor. England was offering Texas great inducements to get a naval base at Galves-

ton. Once fortified there, and in league with Texas,
England would have planted herself squarely across the
path of Southern advance. Houston had about exhausted
his influence with the Texas Legislature. New England
opposition to annexation was about to throw Texas into
the arms of Great Britain. A man was dispatched by
Houston from Nacogdoches, then the Capital of Texas,
on horseback, to Jackson at Nashville, Tenn., to inform
Jackson that if Congress hesitated any longer the treaty
with England would become a fact. Jackson rushed a
messenger on horseback to Louisville, Ky., then up the
Ohio to Pittsburgh, thence to Washington, and at the
last moment thwarted New England and prevailed on
Congress to agree to the annexation of Texas. How
absurd it is for any Southerner, in view of these facts,
especially any Texan, to sing the hymn of Dr. Smith—

"My country, 'tis of thee,
 Sweet land of liberty,
   Of thee I sing!
 Land where my fathers died,
   Land of the *Pilgrims' pride*," and so on.

Neither Dr. Smith, nor any of his people, had any
"pride" in the South, and so far from having any pride
in Texas, they were moving heaven and earth to keep it
from becoming a part of our "country." It is a fact,
whether you like for it to be told or not. When that
song is sung in my home, I always teach my children to
substitute the word "Patriot" for the word "Pilgrim."
Respect for those rugged old Pilgrims who were trying
to get up out of their graves to prevent Texas from
coming into the Union forbids that we should include
that fair land in the "My country" of Dr. Smith's song.

[ 47 ]

## THE SOUTH WAS RIGHT.

Every step of Southern expansion to the Pacific was bitterly opposed by the North. Deny it, who can!

Now, there was no such hostility on the part of the South toward Northern expansion. On the contrary, Virginia gave to the North a territory almost the size of Texas. When the War of the Revolution closed, Virginia had a valid claim to "the Northwest Territory." But with patriotic devotion to the whole country she ceded her claim to the newly made Union; and out of that territory was formed the great States of Ohio, Indiana, Illinois, Michigan and Wisconsin, so that Virginia won the proud title from the patriotic heart of America in the good old days of "Mother of States and of statesmen." But this generosity was soon forgotten in the growing hostility to the whole South.

This hostility of the North expressed itself, secondly, in the persistent attack on the local institutions of the South, and especially of slavery. They began, and maintained, a systematic anti-slavery agitation. They held public meetings to denounce the South and political conventions to organize against it. They printed numberless papers and pamphlets devoted to stirring up and educating Northern public sentiment to hate the South. They secretly circulated documents throughout the South inciting the slaves to revolt. They formed societies and parties to make war on the Southern system of social life. They employed the most gifted orators to address the masses and fire their passions against the Southern people. By speech and pen, in ten thousand ways, they pushed their hostile crusade against the South. Finally it culminated in its natural and proper result in the attempt of John Brown to incite a race war among the Southern slaves. John Brown was an anarchist. Yet he was a hero in the North because he impersonated the general feeling of hostility to the South. He is a hero still, as for that. They build costly monuments to keep his memory safe, when it ought to rot in eternal oblivion. In his famous Cooper Institute speech Mr. Lincoln said this about John Brown's mad invasion of Virginia: "That affair, in its philosophy, corresponds with the many attempts at the assassination of kings and emperors. An enthusiast ventures the attempt which ends in little else than his own execution." This estimate of Lincoln, which I believe is correct, put John Brown in the class of Gitteau, the insane wretch who murdered Garfield. According to Lincoln, it is the "soul" of an assassin that "goes marching on," and monuments are erected and peans sung to the arch anarch of our history. Lincoln classed John Brown with J. Wilkes Booth, his own assassin. The North honors Brown and damns Booth! Can any one wonder that the South felt that her most sacred rights were in danger when the North applauded John Brown as a national hero, and held him up as a glorified "martyr" and representative of the spirit and purposes of the North? What might we not expect when the political party that claimed him as its forerunner acquired the vast powers of the Federal government!

The hostility of the North is seen in the continued misrepresentation and defamation of the Southern people. I need cite only one example. It is by one of their greatest men, on whose memory, when he died, our own great Lamar, sounding the first note of returning fraternity over the subsiding floods of sectional hatred, pronounced a noble eulogy. If such a man could use such violent, intemperate, vulgar, and insulting speech

[ 49 ]

on the floor of the United States Senate, what might not
be expected from speakers who neither knew or cared
for the ethics of public discussion? I refer to the speech
of Charles Sumner on "The Crime Against Kansas,"
which provoked the assault of Preston S. Brooks, member of Congress from South Carolina. Every sentence
is vituperative. Every epithet is vitriolic. The whole
speech is an irruption of vulgar malice. To use his own
language, he "discharged the loose expectoration of his
speech" upon the South and her people. While it was
an unfortunate thing, I do not wonder that Brooks
chastised him. There is a limit to the license of abuse.
Human nature can stand so much and no more, and
Sumner went far over the line. But as in the case of
John Brown, the North hailed in Sumner an exponent
of her sentiments and denounced Brooks as "a cowardly
assassin" and his State as a barbarous people. In doing
this they made the speech of Sumner an expression of
Northern sentiment; and if that speech does not slander
the South I do not know the difference between light
and darkness. It smells of brimstone!

I said one example of this misrepresentation would
serve my purpose, but I must cite another, and a far
more influential one. I mean the book, "Uncle Tom's
Cabin," by Mrs. Harriet Beecher Stowe. Before the
West was settled the wide prairies were covered with
luxuriant grass. After a long season of rainless weather
a match carelessly thrown into the dry stubble would
start a conflagration that would sweep in flaming fury
over the whole country. Nothing could stop it, or stand
before it. It carried ruin and death to man and beast
in its path and left a blackened desert behind it. I can
think of nothing that so appropriately illustrates the

effect of Mrs. Stowe's book on the public opinion of the world. It was a lighted match thrown into the dry stubble of the world's thought and set it on fire. Millions of people, who would never read a political speech, or care for the argument of statesmen, read this vile book, and got the idea that the Southern people were a set of wicked barbarians, whose chief delight was in hunting runaway slaves and inflicting tortures upon them. Of course, the book was false to the core; but the millions who read it believed it was true.

Over yonder in the church, visible from where I sit, there is a marble tablet on the wall. The inscription on it tells us that it is sacred to the memory of Bishop William Capers, of the Methodist Episcopal Church, South. Among many other things for which his memory is revered is the fact that he was "the founder of the missions to the slaves." So at the very time that Mrs. Stowe was writing her libellous account of slavery, and making millions believe the Southern people were little better than savages, and investing her slanders with the romantic charms of a pharasaical philanthropy, Southern ministers of the Gospel, led by this godly Bishop, were telling these poor benighted Negroes, torn from their native land by Yankee cupidity, the story of a Savior's love, and leading thousands of them to faith in Christ. Not one word does Mrs. Stowe tell of this missionary work among the slaves of the South. Her purpose was to blacken and defame us, and she succeeded in doing it. Her book, "translated into every civilized tongue, became world literature." The effect of this book in England in preventing the recognition of the Confederacy was very great. General Charles Francis Adams says: "There was but one way of accounting for it.   Uncle Tom and Legree were respectively doing their work.   So it was that *The Index* (a paper that was pro-Southern) despairingly at last declared: 'The emancipation of the negro from the slavery of Mrs. Beecher Stowe's heroes is the one idea of the millions of British who know no better and do not care to know.'   Like the Cherubim with the flaming sword, this sentiment stood between Lancashire and cotton, and the inviolate blockade made possible the subjugation of the Confederacy.   With Pyrrhus, it was a tile thrown by a woman from a housetop; with Lee it was a book issued by a woman from a printing press! The missiles were equally fatal."

When you calmly reflect on all this, you will doubtless admit that the South had good reason to be alarmed. The North was growing more powerful all the time, and its spirit more aggressive and intolerant.   The hostility to the South, and stern determination to interfere with its domestic condition, Constitution or no Constitution, justified the South in seeking to protect itself by resorting to the legal right of secession.   At any rate, the vast majority believed that their rights were no longer safe in a Union controlled by such hostility.

But even more than by this hostility, the South was influenced by the attitude of the North toward the Constitution.

The Constitution was the basis of the Union.   To attack that was to attack the foundation.   To ignore it was to throw down all the barriers to tyranny, and in the place of constitutional government to erect an irresponsible despotism.   That is exactly what the North did.   I affirm, and will prove, that the North spurned and repudiated the Constitution. They denounced it and they disobeyed it.

They denounced it. Here is the proof:

Wm. H. Seward, one of their foremost men, and afterward one of Lincoln's cabinet, said: "There is a higher law than the Constitution which regulates our authority over the domain. Slavery must be abolished, and we must do it." Charles Sumner said: "The fugitive slave act is filled with horror; we are bound to disobey this act."

William Lloyd Garrison said: "The Union is a lie. The American Union is an imposture, a covenant with death and an agreement with hell. We are for its overthrow! Up with the flag of disunion, that we may have a free and glorious republic of our own."

Joshua R. Giddings said: "I look forward to the day when there shall be a servile insurrection in the South; when the black man, armed with British bayonets, and led on by British officers, shall assert his freedom and wage war of extermination against his master. And, though we may not mock at their calamity nor laugh when their fear cometh, yet we will hail it as the dawn of a political millennium."

Anson P. Burlingame said: "The times demand and we must have an antislavery Constitution, an antislavery Bible, and an antislavery God."

This proof might be extended indefinitely; but these testimonies from representative men is sufficient. They express the true sentiment of the North, and disclose an utter contempt for the Union on the basis of the Constitution.

They disobeyed the Constitution. Here is the proof:

# THE SOUTH WAS RIGHT.

The Constitution recognized the right of property in slaves and protected it. If it had not done so, those States where slavery existed when the Union was formed would never have entered it. Now there were four million slaves in the South, and they represented at the lowest computation a billion dollars' worth of property. Of course slavery was an evil. All recognized that. But the North was as responsible for it as the South. While it was an evil, it was not all evil. As a rule the Negroes were treated kindly, and cruel treatment was the exception. The unanswerable proof of this is the fact that during the war the great mass of the slaves were faithful to their masters, and helped us in the struggle, and many after they were free, preferred to stay with "their people" to going with their liberators. It had its benefits for the slave, too, for it trained ignorant Africans to habits of civilized life, and was a great industrial school for the race. All of this did not justify the institution of slavery, but it did mitigate its evil, and give the lie to the Northern statements about it. It was easy to say it ought to be abolished. Multitudes in the South believed that, and but for the unwarranted interference of the North, it is highly probable the way would have been found for the gradual liberation of the slaves. General Lee liberated some Negroes belonging to his family while the war was going on. But right or wrong, the South had over a billion dollars invested in this form of property, and it was protected by the Constitution. Besides the whole social, civic and industrial life of the South was inextricably intertwined with the institution of slavery. To suddenly liberate the slaves was to wreck civilization in the South, and do more harm than good, as was amply demonstrated when the North finally did it by the power of the sword. Now the cold-blooded purpose of the North was, Constitution or no Constitution, to suddenly destroy this vast property without compensation to the owners, and turn loose these four million ignorant Negroes as free people upon the South. But to the proof that the North disobeyed the Constitution.

Section 2, of Article IV, of the Constitution, says: "No person held to Service or Labor, in one State, under the laws thereof, escaping into another State, shall, in consequence of any Law or Regulation therein, be discharged from such Service or Labor, but *shall be delivered up* (italics mine) on Claim of the Party to whom such Service or Labor may be done."

This is the law which no less a man than Charles Sumner said, "We are bound to disobey" it. To quote Dr. Curry on this point: "Ten Northern States, with impunity, with the approval of such men as Governor Chase, afterward Secretary of the Treasury under Mr. Lincoln and Chief Justice of the Supreme Court, nullified the Constitution, declared that its stipulation in reference to the reclamation of fugitives from labor was a 'dead letter,' and to that extent they dissolved the Union, or made an *ex parte* change in the terms upon which it was formed. These States did not formally secede, but of themselves, without assent of those Mr. Jefferson described as 'coparties with themselves to the compact,' changed the conditions of union and altered the articles of agreement." In short, though the Constitution expressly agreed that fugitive slaves should be given up, the North deliberately said they shall not. If that was not disobeying the Constitution, I confess I am incapable of understanding in what disobedience consists. Of course, if they could declare one part of the Constitution "a dead letter" because it did not suit them, they could abrogate any part of it for the same reason.

In 1850, only two years before his death, Daniel Webster, Senator from Massachusetts, made a speech which became known as "The Seventh of March Speech." I once heard Mrs. Mary A. Livermore, of Boston, deliver her really great lecture on "Wendell Phillips and His Times." She boasted that she was one of the original Abolitionists, and stood by the side of Wendell Phillips when he faced the mobs to plead for the liberation of the "cruelly oppressed slave." Referring to Webster's Seventh of March Speech, she said that up to that time Webster was the idol of New England. They were proud of his fame and felt that in him the Nation had a champion that no foe would care to meet, or meeting, would rue it forever. But after that speech, the idol was toppled in the dust, and the admired champion had proved a recreant coward. She said the first effect on reading it was a sort of dazed amazement, which was succeeded by a sickening revulsion, and that by a violent indignation, and Webster was thenceforth regarded as a "traitor" who had betrayed the nation's trust.

Mr. Bryan says, in a note on this speech in his "The World's Famous Orations," "Curtis, the biographer of Webster, admits that this speech met with general disfavor throughout the North." Schurz describes the antislavery men as contemplating "the fall of an archangel." Webster was called " a recreant son of Massachusetts," "a fallen star," and "a bankrupt politician gambling for the presidency," while Whittier, in one of his poems, wrote:

# THE SOUTH WAS RIGHT.

"All else is gone; from those great eyes
      The soul is fled;
When faith is lost, when honor dies,
      The man is dead.

Then pay the reverence of old days
      To his old fame;
Walk backward with averted gaze
      And hide his shame!"

Poor Webster! And what was it that the North called
"his shame?" What was it that the enlightened North,
shuddering with horror at the sin of slavery, thought
put out the light of Webster's "great eyes," exiled his
"soul" and slew his "honor?" It was Webster's fidelity
to the Constitution! It was his conscientious obedience
to an oath which was equally binding upon every American citizen. Fidelity to one's oath is, among all civilized people, regarded as an essential attribute of honor;
but the North denounced this as "shame" in Webster,
and called him "a fallen archangel" because he kept
faith with his oath. If that was not putting darkness
for light I will give it up. Let us see what Webster
said, that we may clearly understand how completely
the North, in its rage against the South, had repudiated
the basic principles of political morality on which the
Union was founded. Here is what he said: "But I
will allude to other complaints of the South, and especially to one which has, in my opinion, just foundation;
and that is, that there has been found at the North,
among individuals and among legislators, a disinclina-
tion to perform fully their constitutional duties in
regard to the return of persons bound to service who
have escaped into the free States. In that respect, the

South, in my judgment, is right, and the North is wrong. Every member of every Northern Legislature is bound by oath, like every other officer in the country, to support the Constitution of the United States; and the article of the Constitution which says to these States that they shall deliver up fugitives from service, is as binding in honor and conscience as any other article. No man fulfils his duty in any Legislature who sets himself to find excuses, evasions, escapes, from this constitutional obligation. I have always thought that the Constitution addressed itself to the Legislatures of the States or to the States themselves. It says that those persons escaping to other States "shall be delivered up," and I confess I have always been of the opinion that it was an injunction upon the States themselves. When it is said that a person escaping into another State, and coming therefore within the jurisdiction of that State, shall be delivered up, it seems to me the import of the clause is, that the State itself, in obedience to the Constitution, shall cause him to be delivered up. That is my judgment. I have always entertained that opinion, and I entertain it now."

That was clear and true and brave. Yet the saying it, probably, cost Webster the prize of the presidency of the United States, and the North regarded him as "a fallen archangel." The reference to fallen archangels suggests a different construction to me. If to stand firm for the truth amidst universal rebellion against it, if to be loyal to one's allegiance when all others are throwing it off, if to keep faith with conscience—if this be noble, then Webster in the United States Senate on the seventh of March, 1850, reminds me of one higher than an archangel; the Seraph,

## THE SOUTH WAS RIGHT.

"Abdiel, faithful found
Among the faithless, faithful only he;
Among the innumerable false, unmoved,
Unshaken, unseduced, unterrified,
His loyalty he kept, his love, his zeal;
Nor number, nor example, with him wrought
To swerve from truth, or change his constant mind,
Though single."

But this bitterness toward Webster emphasizes the attitude of the North toward the Constitution. To quote Dr. Curry again, in his "Civil History of the Government of the Confederate States," a book, by the way, that ought to be read by every one who desires to understand the truth about the War for the Union, "The Northern States, not in the regular prescribed form, but in the most irregular, illegal, and contemptuous manner, by ecclesiastical action and influence, by legislative and judicial annulment, by public meetings, by pulpit and press, by mobs and conspiracies and secret associations, made null and void a clear mandate of the Constitution, protective of Southern property, and adopted as an indispensable means for securing the entrance of the Southern States into the Union." They disobeyed the Constitution.

Now in 1860 Mr. Lincoln was elected President by the party that had for twenty-five years fostered this hostility to the South and gloried in this disobedience to the Constitution. What more reasonable than to suppose that the principles of the party would control the policy of the administration? Can any one wonder or blame the South for taking steps to protect itself from the danger that menaced it? They must do it in the Union or out of it. For an honorable people this

[ 59 ]

offered no alternative. They had no right while remaining in the Union to resist its authority; but they had the legal right to withdraw from the Union, and since the government had now passed into the hands of a party bent on the destruction of Southern rights, they were fully justified in the step of secession.

I think Lincoln was a sincere man, and honestly felt it to be his duty to resort to arms; but he was the chosen candidate of a party that had proclaimed its virtual independence of the Constitution. And did not Lincoln soon show that he was in full accord with his party, so far as the constitutional limitations on his authority were concerned? What constitutional right did he have to call for troops to invade the South? "If he could do that, he could do anything." Virginia evidently thought so. She voted down secession until Lincoln's call for troops. That ended all debate, for if he could do that he could do anything. And he did do a world of things without warrant of law. He justified his course on the ground that it was necessary "to save the Union." Here is his language: "I felt that measures otherwise unconstitutional might become lawful by becoming indispensable to the preservation of the Constitution through the preservation of the nation. Right or wrong, I assumed this ground, and I now avow it." That was heroic, and success made it patriotic; but if it was not revolutionary I have yet to learn the meaning of the word. It was the bold assumption of autocratic and illegal power under the plea of public necessity, which we denounce as tyranny in Napoleon and applaud as patriotism in Lincoln. A man knows very little of human nature who would expect an intelligent, high-spirited, and liberty-loving people, such as the Southern people of that generation were, to yield one iota to such tyrannical authority. To resist it to the utmost became the sacred duty of every freeman.

But Lincoln and his party did unconstitutional things which they could not justify on the ground of military necessity, such, for example, as the admission of West Virginia into the Union. What warrant of law did they have for that? According to the theory of the Union, which they had a million of men in arms to enforce, a State could not secede. Virginia had not withdrawn from the Union, and those of her citizens who were resisting the Federal government were in rebellion. The relation of the State of Virginia to the Union, therefore, was exactly what it was before its claim to have left it. So when they divided Virginia they divided a State which was as much in the Union as Ohio. Where was the authority for that? The truth is they had neither law nor precedent, nor the excuse of military necessity; it was pure, unadulterated despotism—the right of the sword. West Virginia is the bastard of the Union, conceived in sin and born in iniquity. And its admission into the Union contradicted all the North had proclaimed about secession, for while they hurled a million men against the South to prevent the secession of Virginia, and justified it on the ground that secession was a political heresy utterly ruinous to the American Union, they allowed West Virginia to secede from Virginia. West Virginia is the monumental proof that the North in 1860 had thrown the Constitution to the winds, and ruled the country as a despotism. The South may be overthrown, but it may be counted on to resist such lawless exercise of power as long as Anglo-Saxon blood flows in her veins.

## THE SOUTH WAS RIGHT.

I have said far more than enough to prove my point, and will only make a brief reference to the despotism of the North after the close of the war. Even so fair and conservative a judge as General Charles Francis Adams says: "As an historic fact, the Constitution was then suspended. It was suspended by an act of an irresponsible Congress, exercising revolutionary but unlimited powers over a large section of the common country." I think General Adams' words apply to Congress from the day the Republican party assumed the powers of government. As a political party it was utterly lawless.

I conclude, therefore, that the Southern States had the right to secede in 1860, that the circumstances fully justified them in appealing to that right for protection against the hostility of the North; and that the North had no constitutional right to coerce the seceded States to return to the Union, but appealed to the right of revolution to force upon the States a new and different construction of the Constitution from its original meaning. * * * * * *

Whether the North was justified in this revolution or not; whether a national government, with its highly centralized power, is a better form of government than the federal republic contemplated by Washington and his compatriots; whether republican institutions and the principles of popular government are compatible with the imperialistic character implicit in the present organization of the national government—these are questions that are outside of this discussion. Neither am I concerned with the merits of the doctrine of secession. That has nothing to do with the case. My single aim has been to show that the right of secession existed in

# THE SOUTH WAS RIGHT.

1860, and to explain the reasons why the Southern people resorted to it for self-protection against the North.

The American Union has been aptly likened to the solar system, in which the stability and harmony of the system depends on the balance of the centripetal and centrifugal forces. If the centripetal force overbalances the centrifugal, the planets will fall into the sun, and ruin will ensue. If the centrifugal overbalances the centripetal, the planets will fly apart, and the system will be wrecked. As applied to the Union, the national idea represents the centripetal force, and the doctrine of State's rights represents the centrifugal force, and the perpetual problem of statesmanship is to maintain these forces in equal balance. If the national principle is carried too far, it will destroy the State and the government will become a centralized despotism. If the principle of State's right be carried too far, it will dissolve the Union and involve everything in chaos. It is one of the wonders of political history, and one of the noblest evidences of the capacity of the American people for self-government, that the Constitution survived the shock of the war, and after having been completely suspended for a time, has again become the paramount authority in the Nation. Nor is there any sign of the times more encouraging to the heart of the patriot than the political philosophy which expresses the new national consciousness in the maxim, "An indissoluble Union of indestructible States." The integrity of the State is as essential to the Nation as the solidarity of the Union.

When the Americans resolved not to submit to British oppression, Pitt exclaimed: "I glory in the resistance of America. Three million Americans who would submit to the unjust measures of the British Ministry would be fit instruments with which to enslave the rest." Looking back over the history of our country, so far from condemning the South for her course in 1860, I glory in her resistance to the North. A people who would have submitted to the lawless and unconstitutional acts of the Republican party of that period could never have made the magnificent country we have today. The baptism of blood consecrated the whole nation. Each side learned to respect the other for the earnestness of their convictions and the courage with which they maintained them. Both sides are satisfied with the final adjustment.

Does any one ask why this discussion, if all are satisfied with the result? If the issues were definitely and forever settled, why not let the curtain fall. and the whole subject pass into a happy oblivion? There are three reasons for not forgetting the past.

First, though the issues were settled, the principles remain and are as vital today as they were then. America has not yet solved her political problems, and from no period of her history has she more or more important lessons to learn than from the great struggle for constitutional government of these United States. No such Republic as ours ever existed before.

A second reason is that an appreciation of the past is the inspiration of the present. A great man has told us "that no people who are indifferent to what their ancestors did are likely to do anything for which their posterity will have reason to be proud." The present is the product of the past. The men, both in the North and the South, who are the leaders in the splendid progress of today are men who have drunk deep at the fountain of their country's history. Patrick Henry was right when he said: "I have but one lamp by which

my feet are guided; and that is the lamp of experience.
I know of no way of judging the future but by the
past." A flippant disregard for the past is the sure
sign of a fool. When a man, prominent in political life,
said in his rancid book, "The Southerner," "About the
Confederacy and the war I cared not a rap," he made a
sorry spectacle of his lack of self-respect, to say nothing
of his lack of respect for history. The idea of a sensible man saying he does not care "a rap" for the stu-
pendous event in American history, the War for the
Union! One wonders how he ever climbed so high with
such a narrow mind.

A third reason is a sacred reverence for the memory
of the dead. They were bone of our bone and flesh of
our flesh. From them we received our earthly being.
They poured out their life-blood for our sake. To what
lower degree of baseness could we sink than to forget
them, and let the sordid concerns of a material pros-
perity obliterate the sentiment that reveres them.
What more ignoble cowardice could we show than to
allow the youth of the South to quietly imbibe the opinion that, if not traitors to their country, they were
deluded and reckless revolutionists! Could we more
effectually renounce our claim to be patriots than to
quench the hallowed fire of admiration for them as the
martyrs of liberty! Perish the thought that it is possible to forget them as long as their blood shall flow
in our veins!

> "Where shall their dust be laid?
> On the mountain's starry crest,
> Whose kindling lights are signals made
> To the mansions of the blest:

[ 65 ]

## THE SOUTH WAS RIGHT.

No, no, no!
For bright though the mountain be,
It has no gem in its diadem
Like the life-spark of the free!

"Where shall their dust be laid?
  On the ocean's stormy shore,
With wailing woods at their backs arrayed,
  And shouting seas before:
      No, no, no!
For, deep as its waters be,
They have no depth like the faith which fired
The martyrs of the free!

"Where shall their dust be laid?
  By the valley's greenest spot,
As it ripples down, in leaps of shade,
  To the blue forget-me-not:
      No, no, no!
For, green as the valley be,
It has no flower like the bleeding-heart
Of the heroes of the free!

"Or where muffled pageants march,
  Through the spired and chiming pile,
To the chancel-rail of its oriel arch,
  Up the organ-flooded aisle:
      No, no, no!
For, grand as the minsters be,
They could never hold all the knightly hosts
Of Jackson and of LEE!

"Where shall their dust be laid?
  In the urn of the Human Heart,

## THE SOUTH WAS RIGHT.

Where its purest dreams are first displayed,
  And its passionate longings start:
    Yes, yes, yes!
  By memory's pictured wave,
  Is a living shrine for the Dead we love,
  In the land they died to save."

We read in the classic legends of old Rome that there was an earthquake which opened a wide chasm in the very heart of the city. The people tried in vain to fill it up. At last an oracle declared it would never be filled until the most precious thing in Rome was thrown into its depths. A brave young man, Marcus Curtius, hearing the oracle, said that courage was the most precious thing in Rome. He clad himself in full armor, mounted his steed, and calling aloud upon the gods to witness that he devoted himself to his country's weal, he made his horse leap into the yawning gulf. The legend declared that the chasm instantly closed. A greater chasm rent the mighty republic of America than ever cracked the foundation of Rome. The people tried in vain to fill it up. It would not close until the most precious thing in the republic, the glorious manhood of America, was thrown into its depths. Legions of noble men, the flower of the North and South alike, like Marcus of old, clad in full armor, leaped into its yawning abyss, and the bloody chasm closed above them forever.

So may it be with our great republic!

CPSIA information can be obtained
at www.ICGtesting.com
Printed in the USA
BVHW041131120720
583443BV00003B/384

9 781375 844680